N
W
E
S

The GIFT of FREEDOM

How Harriet Tubman Rescued Her Brothers

written by GLENNETTE TILLEY TURNER illustrated by LAURA FREEMAN

Abrams Books for Young Readers • New York

Harriet Tubman stood by the Big House's gate singing:

I'm sorry I'm going to leave you,
Farewell, oh farewell.
But I'll meet you in the morning,
Farewell, oh farewell.
I'll meet you in the morning,
I'm bound for the Promised Land.
On the other side of Jordan,
I'm bound for the Promised Land.

Harriet then sprinted away. She knew that someone she could trust would hear her song and let her husband and family know she was leaving.

Harriet had been born in Dorchester County on Maryland's Eastern Shore. Her widowed master was drowning in debt and already advertising those she had enslaved for sale in the newspaper. Harriet knew she might not have another chance to run away.

But Harriet did not set out blindly. Always a keen observer, she had learned to use the North Star for a compass, to tell time by the stars, and to find her way by natural signs as well as any hunter could. She could navigate dense forests, locate waterways in the area, and identify the white Quakers and black mariners willing to help enslaved people escape.

So, she fled from Dorchester County and headed north. She was able to avoid slave hunters, and with the help of members of the Underground Railroad, Harriet succeeded in reaching Philadelphia and freedom. She found work there with the abolitionists of the Pennsylvania Anti-Slavery Society, alongside its executive director, William Still.

For the first time ever, Harriet received pay for her labor. But freedom was bittersweet. Her family and friends were still in shackles, and she was far away from the husband she loved. Harriet had already risked her own life to get north. She was prepared to risk it again for the sake of those she had left behind.

Soon after Harriet's arrival in Philadelphia, a man reported news of an enslaved woman and her two children about to be sold in Maryland. Harriet learned that the woman was her own niece and vowed to rescue them. From a safe hiding place in Baltimore, she did. Soon after, Harriet helped plan the escape of three other Freedom Seekers: her brother Moses and two other men.

Harriet decided to help *whoever* would go north. She would lead them to freedom. She gathered group after group of Freedom Seekers and guided their passage to Philadelphia.

But she never forgot her husband and family in Maryland's Eastern Shore. In the years between 1852 and the beginning of 1854, she tried to rescue them two times. Both attempts were unsuccessful, but Harriet did not give up.

On Christmas 1854, Harriet returned to the Eastern Shore again, hoping to give three of her brothers the best possible gift—the gift of freedom!

The man who had enslaved them planned to sell her brothers Ben Jr., Robert, and Henry over the holiday. Her brothers had tried to escape before but were always forced to turn back. This might be their last chance.

Harriet sent a coded letter telling of her plans to Jacob Jackson, a literate black man in Dorchester County. But Jackson was under watch for possible connections to recent escapes. The strange letter raised suspicion, and the police set off to question Jackson. He tossed the letter aside and insisted he didn't understand a word of it. But in reality, he *had* understood its message, so as soon as the police were gone, he hurried to let Harriet's brothers know the news.

Harriet arrived on Christmas Eve. Her timing was perfect. Enslaved workers were often allowed to visit relatives during the holidays. Since Harriet's parents, Ben Sr. and Rit, who lived in nearby Caroline County, were expecting their sons for Christmas dinner, the men's absence would not raise any suspicion. Time was now of the essence. Advertisements had been posted, and the brothers would be sold at public auction the day after Christmas.

Ben Jr. and Henry waited with Harriet near their parents' cabin. But Robert hadn't arrived. Harriet didn't know that Robert's wife was about to deliver their third child.

Robert knew that Harriet wouldn't wait for anyone once a plan was set in motion. So as soon as his daughter was born, he rushed to join Harriet and their brothers. He planned to return for his family at a later time.

It was Christmas morning when Robert reached the prearranged meeting place—a corn crib outside of his parents' cabin. The little band of Freedom Seekers had grown to include Ben Jr.'s fiancée and two more men.

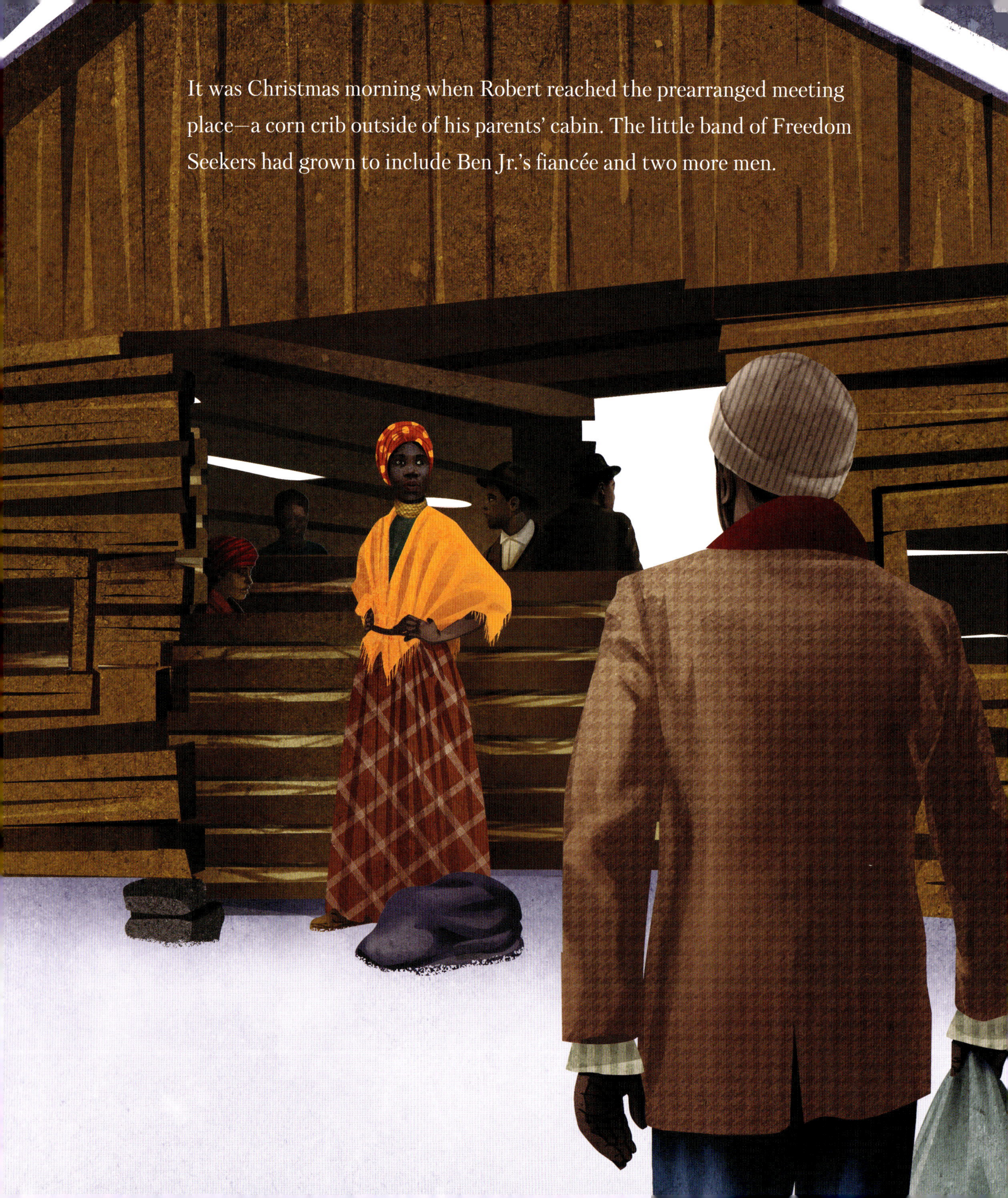

Beforehand, Harriet had been able to alert her father, Ben Sr., to their plans. On Christmas Day, he made several trips to the corn crib to bring them food, making sure to avert his eyes. He knew the slave catchers would question him. He wanted to be able to truthfully say that he had not seen his sons.

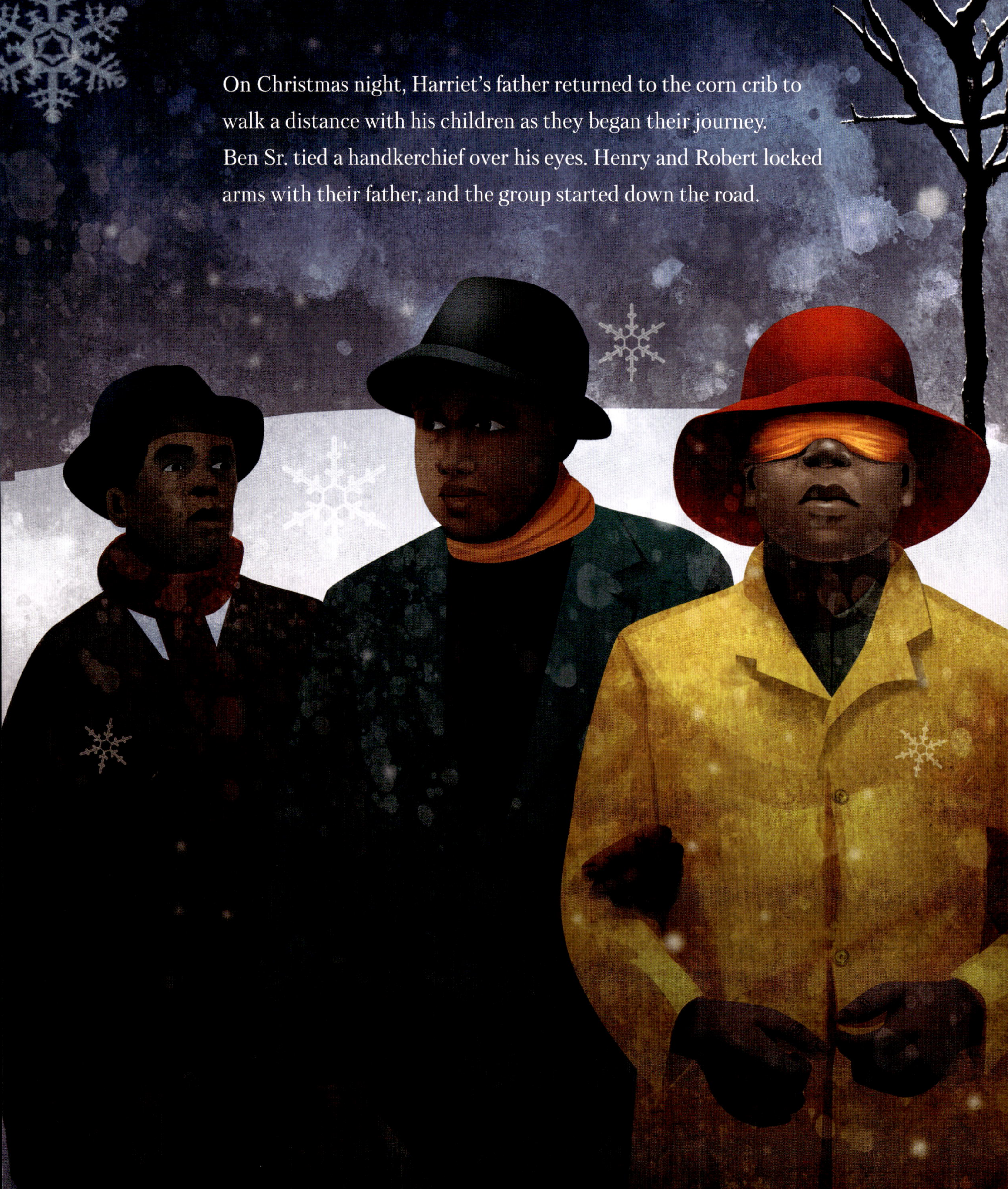

On Christmas night, Harriet's father returned to the corn crib to walk a distance with his children as they began their journey. Ben Sr. tied a handkerchief over his eyes. Henry and Robert locked arms with their father, and the group started down the road.

When the group passed Ben Sr. and Rit's cabin, Harriet and her brothers sneaked one last look at their mother through the window. She sat by the fireplace, distraught and rocking back and forth in her chair. They couldn't afford the time to stop and comfort her.

After a while, their father said goodbye and wished them well. Ben Sr. stood on the road until he could no longer hear their footsteps. Then he removed his kerchief and returned to his wife.

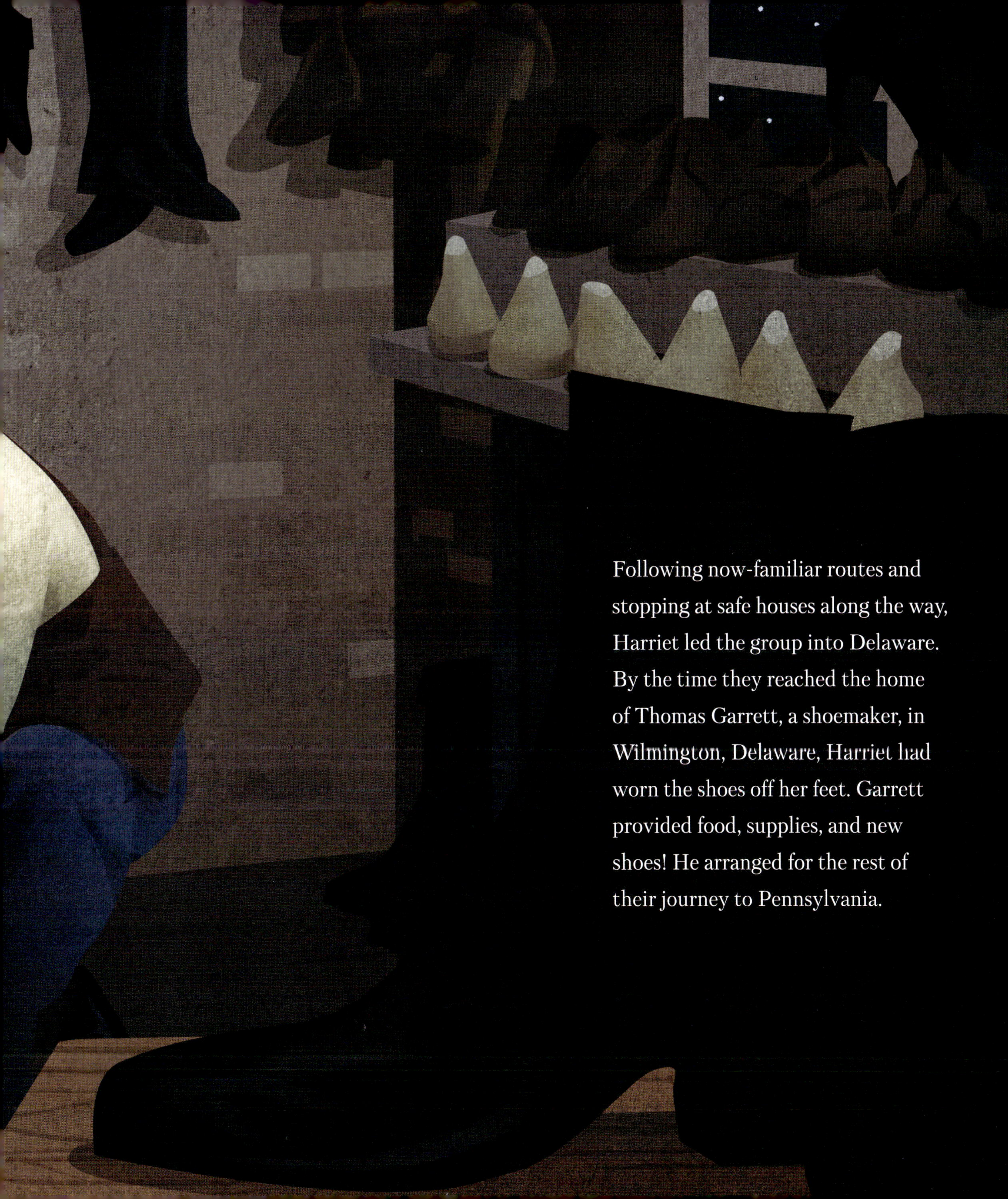

Following now-familiar routes and stopping at safe houses along the way, Harriet led the group into Delaware. By the time they reached the home of Thomas Garrett, a shoemaker, in Wilmington, Delaware, Harriet had worn the shoes off her feet. Garrett provided food, supplies, and new shoes! He arranged for the rest of their journey to Pennsylvania.

Harriet and her Freedom Seekers reached William Still's office in Philadelphia on December 29, after traveling a hundred miles in four days. Knowing that slave hunters would be looking for Harriet's brothers, Still had them take on new identities for their new lives as free men. From that day forward, Ben Jr. would be known as James Stewart. Robert would become John Stewart. Henry became William Henry Stewart.

Philadelphia was no longer the safe haven it had been at the time of Harriet's own escape. William Still arranged for her brothers to board a train to Canada—where they could finally fully embrace Harriet's gift of freedom!

Dear Young Reader,

I have always marveled at (or been amazed by) the seemingly impossible things Harriet Tubman accomplished. And I find the rescue of her brothers to be especially remarkable.

From that time until today, many people have wondered how she was able to do all the things she did. When you think about it, you and I actually know her secret to success. As an enslaved person, although she was denied the opportunity to learn to read and write, she took advantage of every opportunity to learn how to:

- navigate by the stars,
- survive in the wilderness,
- and work with people who could do things she couldn't do.

Two years after using this knowledge in rescuing her brothers, she used it to accomplish another seemingly impossible feat. She returned to Caroline County and rescued her elderly parents.

Let's follow in Harriet Tubman's footsteps by learning all we can about things that are meaningful to us and cooperating with people who know how to do things we don't know how to do.

This can also be our secret to success,

Glennette Tilley Turner

Author's Note

I had the opportunity to interview Mrs. Alice Brickler, the last of Harriet Tubman's relatives to personally know the legendary Underground Railroad conductor.

Mrs. Brickler told me stories that she heard Harriet Tubman tell about her life.

The story of the Christmas rescue of her brothers is especially remarkable. I knew that readers would be as intrigued as I by Harriet Tubman's:

- perfect sense of timing,
- knowledge of what actions she needed to take,
- ability to draw upon the unique talents of fellow Underground Railroad workers,
- and awareness that freedom was the best Christmas gift imaginable.

This was one of the thirteen trips she made to the Eastern Shore, and her brothers were three of the seventy people she is credited with having rescued. She never ceased to plan her missions to fit the situation. When she returned for her elderly parents, she improvised a horse-drawn cart so they could ride.

Sadly, not every one of the Freedom Seekers that Harriet rescued had things work out as they had hoped. For example, Robert was never reunited with his wife.

In addition to the stories of Harriet Tubman's life, Alice Brickler remembered how Harriet would admonish her to "learn, learn all you can, because what you have in your head no one can take away!"

Mrs. Brickler described Harriet Tubman as "a little woman"—yet, just think of the long shadow she cast. Although best known for her Underground Railroad work, Harriet Tubman's remarkable accomplishments did not end there.

During the Civil War, she served as a nurse, a spy, and a recruiter of soldiers. One night, she planned and led a raid that freed seven hundred enslaved African Americans from plantations on the Combahee River in South Carolina—thus becoming the first woman in American history to lead an armed military operation.

Harriet Tubman cared for poor and sick African Americans at her home in Auburn, New York. She was a political activist and an ardent suffragist involved in the women's movement from its inception. Her example has inspired freedom movements around the world.

The National Park Service's National Underground Network to Freedom program is an excellent resource that includes everything from historic sites, guided tours, articles, a story time video series, a virtual trip-planning tool called "Travel with Tubman," and more.

My fascination with the Underground Railroad began with Harriet Tubman. She was the catalyst who inspired my research and writing on the subject, which led to my program being recognized by the National Underground Railroad Network to Freedom program and receiving the Wilbur H. Siebert Award for Outstanding Contributions to the field of the Underground Railroad.

SELECTED BIBLIOGRAPHY

Books

Bradford, Sarah H. *Scenes in the Life of Harriet Tubman.* Auburn, NY: W. J. Moses, 1869.

Clinton, Catherine. *The Road to Freedom.* New York: Back Bay Books, 2005.

Conrad, Earl. *General Harriet Tubman.* Washington, D.C.: Associated Publishers, 1990.

Dunbar, Erica Armstrong. *She Came to Slay: The Life and Times of Harriet Tubman*. New York: 37 Ink, Simon & Schuster, 2019.

Larson, Kate Clifford. *Bound for the Promised Land: Harriet Tubman: Portrait of an American Hero.* New York: Ballantine Books, 2004.

Petry, Ann. *Harriet Tubman: Conductor on the Underground Railroad*, rev. ed. New York: Amistad Press, 2007.

Interviews

Author's interview with Mrs. Alice Brickler, August 23, 1983, at her home in Tallahassee, FL.

Videotaped interview titled "Alice Brickler: Living Link with Harriet Tubman," October 16, 1984, at Black Archives, Florida A&M University, Tallahassee, FL.

For Melody Coleman
—G.T.T.

For Milo, my rock, and all those who never give up in the pursuit of justice
—L.F.

The illustrations for this book were created using Photoshop.

Cataloging-in-Publication Data has been applied for and may be obtained from the Library of Congress.

ISBN 978-1-4197-6929-0
eISBN 979-8-88707-091-9

Edited by Howard W. Reeves
Book design by Heather Kelly

Printed and bound in China
10 9 8 7 6 5 4 3 2 1

ABRAMS The Art of Books
195 Broadway, New York, NY 10007
abramsbooks.com